CAMP WABANNA:
THE EARLY YEARS 1940-1990

LARRY FRYE WITH SHERRY WYNNE TUCKER

WESTBOW
PRESS®
A DIVISION OF THOMAS NELSON
& ZONDERVAN

WestBow Press books may be ordered through booksellers or by contacting:

WestBow Press
A Division of Thomas Nelson & Zondervan
1663 Liberty Drive
Bloomington, IN 47403
www.westbowpress.com
844-714-3454

ISBN: 978-1-6642-7358-0 (sc)
ISBN: 978-1-6642-7357-3 (e)

Print information available on the last page.

WestBow Press rev. date: 08/19/2022

The story of Camp Wabanna is dedicated to the memory of Lawrence and Harriet Frye, and their Christian brothers and sisters at Maryland Avenue Baptist Church and First Baptist Church of New Carrollton, who faithfully gave their time, energy, and finances in support of Reverend Emmans' vision for doing the Lord's work at Camp Wabanna.

FOREWORD

Christian camping has a long and storied history in North America. The idea of worship, praise, and learning among Christian friends in alternative space to a traditional church goes back to the camp meetings and brush arbor meetings of the early nineteenth century. Around the time of the Civil War, pastors and youth workers took their young people to remote locations for renewal and recreation. During the 1880s Baptists, Methodists, and the Salvation Army in the northeastern states purchased forest and lake acreage to administer "fresh air programs" for inner city children in the hot summers. The University of Chicago created programs at the Chautauqua Institute in western New York and the Moody Bible Institute operated summer conferences at Mt. Hermon in Massachusetts and in California. Following World War II, evangelists like Jack Wurtzen and Percy Crawford established camps in the Poconos and the Adirondacks that became world famous.

About the same time that Christian camps were emerging, the bible conference movement became a reality. Beginning with the Niagara and Northfield Conferences, elaborate educational programs were offered every summer to interested adults. These were accompanied by preaching and evangelistic services, special music, and lectures by seminary professors and pastors. The typical Methodist camp meeting site included a central tabernacle ringed by small wooden tents and a central dining hall. Those fortunate enough to find a site on a lake or bay added water sports to their recreation. Famous among the national centers were Ocean Park, Maine; Asbury Park, New Jersey; Green Lake, Wisconsin; River Valley Ranch, Maryland; and Ridgecrest, North Carolina. Thousands of Christian camps adorn the landscapes of the United States and Canada today. Millions of young people and adults are blessed. As the little book shows, Camp Wabanna fits neatly into this great history. The dream of

Rev. W. A. Emmans and the members and friends of Maryland Avenue Baptist

Church in Washington DC (later the United Baptist Church of New Carrollton, Maryland), was realized in their initial camp site on the Rhode River, and later with the purchase of the magnificent property looking out over the convergence of the Rhode and West Rivers into the Chesapeake Bay.

Great singing, bible preaching, delicious food, and warm fellowship has made up the days and evenings at Camp Wabanna for over eight decades. One can still hear the riveting testimony of famed University of Michigan football star and Pocket Testament League evangelist Glenn Wagner, accompanied by the beautiful inspirational chalk artistry of Ding Teuling, and the music ministry of the Homer Phillips Family.

Larry Frye and I are lifelong friends. We grew up as believers in Christ, in two Christian homes. He introduced me to Wabanna in the 1960s and I much enjoyed the conference experiences. Likewise, my wife and her two sisters had great times at the Camp. It is my overwhelming pleasure to provide this forward in honoring my friendship and extending the outreach of Camp Wabanna.

William H. Brackney, B.A. M.A.R., M.A., PH.D.
M. R. Cherry Distinguished Professor *Emeritus* of Christian Thought
Acadia University
Wolfville, Nova Scotia
Class of 1966 Gabriel DuVal Senior High School

OVERVIEW AND THE BEGINNING

Reverend Hal Norton eloquently described Garden City Chapel and Retreat in the 46- page history he wrote entitled, *The Story of Garden City Chapel and Retreat.* His words perfectly describe Camp Wabanna, as well. "It is a beautiful story of faith, vision, sacrifice, love, and service. It is the story of how God has used people from many denominations and many walks of life to do his wonderful work. The great beauty of the story is that it is not the result of one group or group of individuals. The reason for the great success of [Camp Wabanna] is that God laid his hand on it and has never taken his hand away since.

In the following pages many names have been called to make the story personal. There are countless hundreds of other names that could have been called. To all of them, we should be always grateful."

Established in 1941, Camp Wabanna and Retreat Center is a non-profit non denominational Christian ministry which sits on a 23 acre point where the Rhode and West Rivers converge into the Chesapeake Bay. Wabanna ministry encompasses two primary methods of outreach: a summer residential and day camp for boys and girls running from late June to mid-August, and a retreat center offering week and weekend retreat rentals of our property for overnight groups that can range in size from 20 to 232.

Camp Wabanna was founded by Reverend Emmans, who pastored the Maryland Avenue Baptist Church in Washington DC. He along with his wife, Viola, and church congregation raised enough money to purchase a small camp called Callawassee, about three miles away from the site where Camp Wabanna sits today.

The name Camp Wabanna is rooted in the mission of serving children from Washington DC, "wa" Baltimore, "ba" and Annapolis "anna" and exposing them to the transformative power of Christ in a setting different than the cities in which they lived. In 1953 the current property became available and Reverend Emmans was able to purchase it through the generous giving of others. He promised donors an amazing return on their investment: changed lives of those who would be introduced to Christ and grow in their walk with him there throughout the years. Camp Wabanna has remained a ministry that holds to biblical truth and lifestyle as a standard of living. The camping experience continues to be the model for the application and promotion of these principles, helping to achieve the goal of providing an environment that directs people toward the love of Jesus Christ.

— Beth Holm

EVERETT GOLIHEW, 2022, BY A LOG CABIN FROM THE CAMP

Reverend William Emmans was called to be pastor of Maryland Avenue Baptist Church in 1928. The stock market crashed in 1929 and for the next ten years the world plunged into the Great Depression. Then came the start of World War II. Our country was attacked at Pearl Harbor on December 7, 1941.

During Reverend Emmans' first fifteen years as pastor, church services and prayer meetings were extremely important to everyone. Reverend Emmans and his congregation prayed for and ministered to each other and the community. There was very little in the way of financial resources, but there was no shortage of perseverance and faith in our loving God.

It was in the midst of these world-wide storms that Camp Wabanna came to be. Camp Wabanna welcomed the first campers and hosted its first revival meetings in late spring of 1942.

Pearl Harbor---------------------Camp Wabanna opens--------------------D-Day
Dec 7, 1941   spring 1942   June 5, 1944

CAMP WABANNA PIONEERS

---◆---

FAITHFUL AND PATIENT CHRISTIANS

Count it pure joy when you fall into various trials and tribulations,
for the trying of your faith produces patience. Let patience
finish its perfect work in you so that you may be perfect
and complete, lacking in nothing.
James 1:2-4

During the Great Depression and World War II, everyone faced many difficult trials. Families suffered financially and lost fathers, husbands, and sons to the war effort. In spite of the hardships they faced, they were willing to help others. The patience they developed was amazing.

I would like to introduce you to some of these faithful Christian people and share some of their trials.

HOW WAS YOUR TRIAL, MAIZIE SMITH? (1921-2019)

Maizie Smith never knew her mother. Maizie's mother died when she was four months old. She was eight years old when her father died. As an orphan, she was taken in and raised by her aunt and uncle in Orange, Virginia. Maizie remembers how little money they had. At a very young age she helped grow vegetables and canned fruit and vegetables so they could have something to eat all year round. She also remembers how much she hated to see the pigs hanging in the barn after they had been slaughtered.

As the depression eased, she moved to northeast Washington DC with her sister. She graduated from McKinley Tech and then married Johnny Smith. Maizie took on the responsibility of church clerk for Reverend Emmans and Maryland Avenue Baptist Church as a volunteer, a position she would hold for twenty years, from 1942 to 1962. 1942 was the year Camp Wabanna opened. Three months after her son, Johnny Jr. was born, Johnny Sr. was called to serve in the US Army.

I went to visit Maizie in March 2019 and was really surprised to see a picture with Johnny's army medals because right smack in the middle was a Purple Heart. I've known Johnny and Maizie my whole life and never knew he stormed the beach at Normandy on D-Day and was wounded in another battle in the European campaign. Over 2,500 Americans lost their lives on D-Day, a battle that was the single most important battle in defeating the Nazis. "The Lord was good to me. He brought my Johnny home," said Maizie Smith.

Reverend Emmans and the congregation of Maryland Avenue Baptist church prayed for and ministered to Johnny, Maizie, and Johnny Jr., as well as many other families that sent their young men to war.

Maizie and Johnny Smith faced many trials and tribulations. I have always found them to be two of the most patient people I have ever known. I found that to be true of many of the members of Maryland Avenue Baptist church and First Baptist Church of New Carrollton.

I was standing in front of the Westin Hotel in Annapolis in March of 2019. There was a conference of legal students doing mock trials as they prepared for their future. I heard one legal student ask another, "How was your trial?"

I thought, what a great question: How was your trial, Johnny Smith? You jump into the water, rushing to the beach where you would face a firestorm of Nazi machine guns and other weapons, whose sole purpose was to put you and your fellow soldiers in the grave. How intense were your prayers for yourself and your comrades? How intense were your prayers for your beautiful wife and new baby son on the other side of the ocean? How was your trial, Johnny Smith?

MAIZIE AND JOHNNY SMITH

HOW WAS YOUR TRIAL, MILDRED LACY? (1889-1976)

William Lacy (1855 – 1950) was a charter member of Maryland Avenue Baptist Church. He was instrumental in bringing Reverend William Emmans to be the pastor. Reverend Emmans would serve in that capacity for forty years. Mr. Lacy would often invite Reverend and Mrs. Emmans to his farm in Seat Pleasant after church on Sundays. I'm sure some of the earliest conversations about starting a summer camp for children happened at the Lacy Farm.

Mr. Lacy's daughter, Mildred, married Samuel Frye. They had four children: Irene, Lawrence, Wilmer, and Virginia. Sam was working two jobs to support his family. How was your trial, Mildred Lacy?

One summer evening Mildred went to the door to greet two police officers. The two officers had come to bring the shocking news that her husband Sam had been shot and killed during a holdup. Two men came in to rob the store where Sam was working. He refused to give them any money and one of the shot him.

Mildred would have to move back to her father's farm. She would have to help with the chores, as well as raise her four children and her nephew. Mildred is one of the most patient people I have ever known. She was my grandmother, and no matter how much I carried on it never seemed to trouble her. All five of those children grew up to serve the Lord as members of Maryland Avenue Baptist Church and First Baptist Church of Carrollton, and three of them were longtime supporters of Camp Wabanna.

LAWRENCE, MILDRED, WILMER

Good Hope D.C.
Sept. 5th 1874

Prof. O.T. Mason,
Columbian College D.C.

Sir:

Permit me to introduce my young friend Wm H. Lacy, one of my former pupils. You can judge of his character when I inform you that he was baptized at the Second Baptist Church last Sabbath evening. You will find him "faithful and true".

Respectfully

D.C. Fountain

Clerk. P.O. Dept.

In the early years of camp, everyone at Maryland Avenue Baptist Church was excited and wanted to help. In the 1940s Reverend Emmans and William Lacy were two men who had formal bible training. Reverend Emmans taught the men's Sunday school class and William Lacy taught the ladies' Sunday school class.

The ladies' class wanted to do something special for the camp. Now this is special! Those ladies made around one hundred handmade quilts. I have never made a quilt, however, I do know that it takes a long time to make one. And do remember, they were all different and all beautiful! Every one of these quilts was made as a gift to the Lord's work.

LACY SUNDAY SCHOOL CLASS

HOW WAS YOUR TRIAL VIRGIL HERSHBERGER? (1901-1986)

Virgil Hershberger lost his wife when she died suddenly from an illness. He was left to raise his three daughters by himself as a single parent. Virgil's job was to plaster walls and ceilings in homes. This meant mixing the plaster, rubbing it on the walls and ceilings with a trowel, then sanding it smooth before handing the job over to the painters.

No day at work was an easy day for Virgil. He could have easily said he didn't have time for the church or anything else. But Virgil served on the deacon's board for many years when Reverend Emmans was pastor. He was at church every Sunday, prayer meetings on Wednesday, and visitations for Thursday.

I remember one hot summer day when we were building the Key House at Camp Wabanna. Reverend Emmans gave me the job of installing hardware on the doors in all ten rooms. As I walked past one of the rooms, there was Virgil on his hands and knees. He was installing hardwood floors. Perspiration was dripping off his face. Virgil didn't have to do that job. He already had enough to do. He wanted to do it.

Virgil wanted to invest in the Lord's work at Camp Wabanna. He recognized the value of using the camp as a tool for teaching the word of God to men, women, boys, and girls. Whenever I hear the term "sweat equity," I think of Virgil. I have wonderful news for Virgil and all the other men and women who invested their time, money, and labor at Camp Wabanna. Your investments are still producing a great dividend in the lives of men, women, boys and girls.

HOW WAS YOUR TRIAL REMO MOSCATELLI?

Remo Moscatelli's stepfather informed him that after he finished eighth grade he would have to quit school and get a job if he wished to continue living in his house. So he did just that. Remo went to work for Western Union delivering telegrams on a bicycle. He later joined the Navy. After serving four years in the Navy, Remo returned home and was able to again work for Western Union.

While working as a Western Union dispatcher, he became interested in the electronic equipment and learned how to repair the machines. He became a very valuable repairman for the company. He learned his trade pretty much through on-the-job training.

Remo and Alice have been serving the Lord together for over sixty years. Remo became a Sunday school teacher and taught high school and college students, even though he had not had the privilege of going to high school or college himself. Remo and Alice invested both time and money in the church and Camp Wabanna.

I asked Remo to share some of his association with Maryland Avenue Baptist Church and Camp Wabanna.

A lot happened in 1956: Remo Moscatelli and Alice Flowers went on a blind date. They then were engaged for 3 months. They were married August 15th. (2019 will be 63 years). They both went to Maryland Avenue Baptist Church.

1956 Remo was discharged from the Navy.

In 1956 Mr. Emmans came to Alice's parent's home. That is where Remo and Alice lived. Mr. Emmans talked to Remo about Christ. The following Sunday Remo asked the Lord to come into his heart and he went forward in church.

While in Mr. Emman's Sunday School Class we learned about Camp Wabanna. We started going to camp for meetings, fun, and work.

We (Remo and several other men in church) built the wall at Camp Wabanna while working a lot of hours in the hot sun. John McShain, the builder of the Immaculent Conception Catholic Church in D.C, gave Mr. Emmans the large stone slabs that could not be used in working on this church in D.C. The stone slabs that they used weighed between 1, 000 and 2,000 pounds each. A wooden derrick was used to put the slabs in the wall. This group of men mixed their own cement which was a hard job. They did many.

Denise (our daughter) was a waitress at Camp Wabana working very hard to take care of the never ending appetites of the campers at breakfast, lunch, and dinner. Steven (Steve) (our son) was a counselor to groups of boys of different ages. Alice was a counselor to the teen-aged girls in Harmony Hall.

Remo and Alice

Everett Golihew, Remo, and I were on a conference call and both Everett and Remo were remembering building the sea wall. Remo recounted that Mr. John McShane, one of the principal contractors of the Shrine of the Immaculate Conception in Washington DC, had provided the large rocks used to build the wall. Some of the rocks were over two thousand pounds. Remo remembers the crazy contraption they used to lower the rocks down the bank. It was indeed a dangerous operation. They had no power lift of any kind. Everett told how they had to lift the railroad ties onto a truck – also with no power equipment.

Remo gave his time freely to camp for projects and also served as a counselor during the Maryland Avenue Baptist Church Sunday week at camp. I remember Remo as a Sunday school teacher and camp counselor. He was like a Christian first sergeant! He didn't want any of us to step out of line because he took his job seriously and he cared.

Others that worked on the wall were Danny Wine, Steve Yates, Butch Bryant, and Jimmy Ryman.

SEA WALL CONSTRUCTION

The first section of the wall, to prevent erosion, was intended to surround the whole camp. Because of other pressing issues, however, it was never completed. In the 1980s I was working with my dad and we both saw an article in the local paper. It revealed that an engineer was concerned with erosion along the Chesapeake Bay. My dad suggested

I go visit the man in Annapolis. When we met, he agreed to walk around the camp. Bob Emmans, the engineer, and I met at the camp. The engineer said he would get back to us. Two weeks later we received a letter from his office saying we should fill in the holes behind the existing wall and grow grass. We were disappointed because we had hoped for some help from the county in slowing down the erosion.

Two months later we received a big surprise. Our engineer friend had shared his report with some other engineers. They had an amazing offer. They needed an outlet for clean water to be released back into the bay, at a place where it would mix quickly with salt water. Camp Wabanna would be the perfect spot for their project! In exchange for access to the end of the peninsula they would extend the seawall out into the bay toward the West River, build a huge pier for their use, and hook all the buildings up to a new public sewer line at an incredible price. The project would create a quiet water area that we could use for canoes and kayaks. Camp Wabanna would also get an additional finished area next to the beach. That part never happened, however, because it was declared a protected wetland area.

THE CANARD FAMILY

I first remember Jim Canard (1910 – 2000) as the nice man who gave us ice cream as the Maryland Avenue Baptist Church picnic was winding down. He loved his role as the deliverer of the ice cream; you could tell by the smile on his face. He did this for many years.

Jim and his wife Rita, and their family, played a big part in the unity of the church family that moved from Maryland Avenue Baptist to become First Baptist Church of New Carrollton. Jim was the head usher and often the first person to greet members and visitors as they came to

worship. Rita was also deeply involved, serving on the deaconess board and working in Sunday school. They were always ready to serve the church and camp in any way they could. The church also served them in return.

Jim and Rita had several grandchildren. One granddaughter was given her grandmother's name – Rita. Granddaughter Rita was born premature and needed an incubator. Something went terribly wrong and Rita would be blind for the rest of her life. I talked to her dad, Buddy Canard, in the fall of 2020. He told me he was asked if he wanted to sue the hospital for malpractice. He said no, he wasn't. He was very glad she was alive and would be a part of his family. We have also been very happy she was part of our church family.

Record Co.
333-7474

RITA CANARD

for bookings call
301-927-0407

☀ Juldane Record Co.

8037 — 13TH STREET
SILVER SPRING, MARYLAND 20910
301-589-5192

RITA CANARD
JULDANE RECORDS RECORDING ARTIST

Rita Canard, blind since birth, with hazel eyes, blond hair, 5' 4", weighing in at 96 lbs., has so much for the world to see. Rita's handicap of blindness hasn't once stopped her from participating in society. Born in Memphis, Tennessee on February 15, 1953, Rita has spent most of her young life making others happy.

Rita started singing in church at the age of three and in school she was active in the field of music. Her talents included: singing with a combo and The Ike Trio at The Maryland School for the Blind where she was a student. Rita graduated from The Maryland School for the Blind in 1973, with a degree in Medical Transcription and trained at Johns Hopkins Hospital in Baltimore, Maryland.

Rita now resides with her parents of Bladensburg, Maryland and has two brothers and one sister.

Rita's hobbies include: sewing, knitting, bowling, swimming, and playing the piano. She has been hostess to open the annual Flower Shows, in Washington, D.C. Rita won a trophy for being the best navigator at the sports car rallies at Rock Creek Park in Washington, D. C.

Some of Rita's favorite vocalists include: The late Patsy Kline, Lynn Anderson, Sandy Posey, Ronnie Milsap, Conway Twitty, and others.

Rita has appeared with Jerry Reed, Bill Phillips, Webb Pierce, and Mel Street at various times. She won the WISZ Grand Ole Opry 50th Anniversary Country Music Talent Search for the Baltimore, Maryland area.

Rita has recorded three single records to date: "Wounded Pride" and "Rhyming Words" (JMT Records), "Neon Women" and "Tear Store" and "Sunshine Feeling" and "She Goes Right on Loving You" (Juldane Records). After the success with her first record, Rita decided to put together her own band. She has appeared with them at several clubs around the area. Rita has also appeared four times on the "Ramada Hour", on WWVA Radio in Wheeling, West Virginia, the last time being with her own band. She also appeared on The Dave Thomas Show on WKBW-TV in Buffalo, New York. Rita has been interviewed and had her records played on the Country Music, USA radio show that The Voice of America produces for broadcast around the world. She has also appeared at the Capitol Center in Largo, Maryland, as well as The Stardust and the University of Maryland.

JULDANE MUSIC, BMI — BIONIC MUSIC, BMI
SILVER SPRING GROOVE RECORDS

MY LORD KNOWS THE WAY THROUGH THE WILDERNESS

My Lord knows the way through the wilderness,
All I have to do is follow.
Strength for today is mine all the way,
And all I need for tomorrow.
My Lord knows the way through the wilderness,
All I have to do is follow.
<u>Are we Downhearted?</u>
Are we downhearted? No! No! No!
Are we downhearted? No! No! No!
Troubles may come and troubles may go,
We trust in Jesus, come weal or woe.

When I was very young I remember singing these songs at Maryland Avenue Baptist Church. I also remember Melvin Matthews leading the evening singing during worship service. People in the congregation could request their favorite sons and we would sing them as a congregation. *My Lord Knows the Way* and *Are We Downhearted?* were requested often. I was ten years old at the time and these songs did not have much meaning to me, however, to many in the congregation these songs were packed with meaning.

REV. WILLIAM EMMONS (1902-1987) AND MRS. VIOLA EMMONS

Rev. and Mrs. Emmans were without a doubt the spiritual leaders for Camp Wabanna. As members of Maryland Avenue Baptist Church and First Baptist Church of New Carrollton, we were given the opportunity to invest in the Lord's Work. This was a great opportunity for everyone who chose to invest. Many people invested their time, money, and talents in the Lord's work (carpenters, plumbers, painters, counselors, waitresses, office work, etc.).

So what kind of people should we be?
You should live holy lives and serve God.
2 Peter 3:11b-12

As the years passed, many other people from other churches joined us to invest in the Lord's work.

One of the great lessons I learned from Rev. Emmans was that when we recited John 3:16 we should not stop, but keep going through verse 17.

For God so loved the world that He gave his only begotten son
that whosoever believes in Him should not perish but have everlasting life.
For God sent hot His son into the world to condemn the world but
that the world through Him might be saved.
John 3:16-17

This is a lesson today's people need to hear (in 2020). It seems so many people believe the church is about judging them when in truth the church is about bringing them GOOD NEWS. The GOOD NEWS that Jesus has paid the way for them to be part of God's family.

Rev. Emmans had the personality of a great leader. We never felt like we were working for him, although he was absolutely in charge. He led in such a way that you knew that you were working *with* him. We were not working for Rev. Emmans, but all working together with Rev. Emmans for the Lord!

We worked together to serve the Lord at the church of New Carrollton. We all invested financially and worked together to build and maintain the church and the camp. We all worked together to teach children and adults the word of God. We all served other churches and groups that would visit the campgrounds. We all ministered to each other and the New Carrollton community and every child that came through the gates of Camp Wabanna. I believe I speak for everyone who was given these opportunities under the leadership of Rev. Emmans: we are all grateful for the opportunity that we had to invest in the lives of "people." We look forward to the day when we all hear the stories of how God worked in the lives of people who were blessed by the ministry of Maryland Avenue Baptist Church, First Baptist Church, the Northeast Rescue Mission, and Camp Wabanna.

Thank you Rev. and Mrs. Emmans!

After becoming pastor in 1929, Rev. Emmans led his church through the Great Depression as well as ministering to families dealing with fallout for World War II. Rev. Emmans lead the congregation of Maryland Avenue Baptist Church into deeper involvement in the community and people who were hurting by founding Camp Wabanna, the Northeast Rescue Mission, and moving to a new larger church building in New Carrollton.

Rev. Emmans led not only from the pulpit, but with a hammer, saw, and a shovel, mixing concrete. Mrs. Emmans was always right by his side. We would always have many men working on projects on Saturdays. During the week Rev. and Mrs. Emmans would work on projects in the evening, usually just the two of them. Mrs. Emmans had to help Rev. Emmans communicate later in his life when his hearing began to fail.

Trouble came in the 1970s, just after Rev. Emmans retired. A new pastor was called. He seemed to be the right pastor to take over at First Baptist, however, he soon became a problem for the church. He was not honest about his degrees and while being pastor at First Baptist he had gone to Harvard to get a PhD in clinical psychology. After being gone for a year, he came back with his new degree. It was soon discovered that he was never registered at Harvard and never received a degree. He resigned, but when he did many members fell away from the church—people who had been supporting the church and Camp Wabanna. By the grace of God, Camp Wabanna made it through that trial.

REV. WILLIAM EMMANS, STEPHEN FRYE

VIOLA EMMANS

NEW LOCATION

···✦···◆···✦···

NEW CHALLENGES

1953: SISTERS OF ST. JOSEPHS

On May 9, 1953, Sisters of St. Josephs sold land to Wabanna Conference Association, with a $10 down payment and a sale price of $135,000. It wasn't just the land – the property came complete with the lodge and several other buildings. The lodge had a fully equipped kitchen and dish washing room, a large dining area, and a chapel. The upper level only had partitions for the showers and bathrooms.

One of the first projects that Rev. Emmans and his band of volunteers addressed was to partition the upper level into separate rooms for sleeping. From 1941 until 1953 the upper level was one big open dorm used for nuns on retreat.

Rev. Emmans asked his wife, Viola, to give each of the buildings a name. The lodge was Melody Lodge. Other buildings included in the sale were given musical names as well. A two story building that would be a boys' dorm she named The Clef. A long a low building she named The Three Flats, which was also to be used as a boys' dorm. A square single story building, which she named The Key House, would be extended and used for ten single room suites. The purchase of the new property brought a new level of excitement to Camp Wabanna supporters. The new property was so much larger and there was so much more work to be done. Thankfully, more people were willing to step up and support the camp's mission. The next section tells about some of the people; there were many, many more.

Camp Wabanna

"Vacation Spot of the Nation's Capitol"
EDGEWATER, MARYLAND

WASHINGTON ADDRESS
P. O. Box 2120

TELEPHONES:
TR. 1472
UN. 2695

Oct. 29, 1952

Dear Friend:

For nine years, Camp Wabanna has conducted a summer camp for boys and girls. We have had many children from poor homes, broken homes and District Institutions, which have caused us to look at life as never before.

Many of these children, with their younger brothers and sisters who were at home, too young to come to camp, live a life in a world all their own, of whom many of us know absolutely nothing, and concerning whom some have never stopped once to ask the question— Does this mean anything to me? They journey through life unloved and unwanted, a sure prey for every vicious mind and scheme, perverted men and women can imagine. These children have been on our hearts for a long time, but until just recently we have been able to do nothing about it except in the summer months.

Just a short time ago a prominent builder, Mr. J. D. Hedin and several of his personal friends promised to build for us, complete in every detail, a beautiful building, housing at least forty children. This will be the perfect answer in our year-round work. In fact the work was started on the present site, but stopped before having gone too far, due to the opportunity now before us of purchasing one of the finest sites on the Chesapeake Bay.

The price of the new property is $135,000 of which we must raise $60,000 in cash by December 1, the balance of $75,000 to be secured as a first trust. Our plan is to secure 2,400 people who will give $25.00 or more by December 1, 1952. The present camp site will be sold and the amount received used to defray part of the first trust. Your gift will make a happy future for some neglected child. If further information is desired we shall be delighted to furnish the same.

Sincerely hoping we may favorably hear from you,

Very truly yours,

W. A. Emmans

BOB (1924 - 2019) AND BETTY OWEN (1929 - 2011)

I first met Bob Owen when we were building the Key House. Craig and I were holding up a sheet of plywood in the ceiling and Rev. Emmans was nailing it into place. Bob came in and saw Rev. Emmans standing on the ladder and said, "Rev. Emmans, let me help you with that." Rev. Emmans got down off the ladder and Bob Owen took it from there. How befitting that was because years later Bob Owen would be a major help to Rev. Emmans vision for Camp Wabanna. He redefined the role of the board of directors and also brought in some new dynamic Christian men who would lead camp forward in a big way.

During World War II Bob enlisted in the Marines. I know he was involved in some battles in the Pacific campaign, but not the exact battles.

ROBERT OWEN

Bob and Betty moved to New Carrollton in the 1960's. They thought they were moving there so Bob could work at NASA in Greenbelt, Maryland, which he did. (He actually received an award from the President of the United States for his work on the

Apollo project.) However, I believe the Lord had a hand in bringing Bob, Betty, and their family to New Carrollton because Bob was such a force in the Lord's work at Camp Wabanna. They have been such a blessing to the church and Camp Wabanna in so many ways.

The Lord used the Owen family to make the giant leap from being a summer only operation to become a year round operation. Without such a step our camp would probably not be here today. Under Bob's leadership as chairman of the board of directors, the Three Flats and The Clef were replaced with two wonderful, two story dorms. These dorms were heated and air-conditioned. Melody Lodge, now called Emmans Lodge, was upgraded with heat and air-conditioning. Then, to honor Betty, the family donated the Owen Family Farmhouse to camp. What a wonderful tribute to our friend of camp, Betty Owen – a dorm where children would learn about God's love for us and His plan for us as believers in Christ.

LAWRENCE (1916 - 2003 AND HARRIET FRYE (1922 - 2017)

Lawrence Frye came to Maryland Avenue Baptist Church with his grandfather, William Lacy, along with Irene Wilmer and Virginia Frye. They came to NE Washington in a horse and buggy, and took a ferry across the Anacostia River. He was thirteen years old when William Emmans became pastor. His family, like Maizie's, survived the Great Depression by working on his grandfather's farm.

Harriet Reid was in Mobile, Alabama at that time. Her father was working in their family printing business. During the depression, business fell to almost nothing. The Reid family was not able to make it financially. Her family would have to leave family and friends and move to Washington DC, where her father, Harry Reid, was able to get work at the Government Printing Office when Harriet was fourteen.

Harriet became friends with Virginia Frye, who invited her to Maryland Avenue Baptist Church. Harriet met Virginia's brothers, one of whom was Lawrence, and she would sometimes visit the Lacy farm. Lawrence and Harriet became great friends and were later married. Before they could even think about a wedding, however, Lawrence, Wilmer, and Harriet's brother Jimmy were called to take part in World War II. Lawrence was sent to the Pacific, while Wilmer and Jimmy went to Europe. At that point, Harriet decided to join the war effort and joined the Marines. The Lord was good to Harriet, just like Maizie, because all four came home after the war. Lawrence and Harriet were married and served Maryland Avenue Baptist Church and First Baptist Church of New Carrollton for the rest of their lives. Lawrence was a deacon and a trustee. Harriet was a deaconess, a Sunday school teacher, and a Sunday school superintendant.

Soon after they were married, Lawrence and Harriet purchased a small flower business in Washington DC. In 1956 Rev. Emmans came to visit the flower shop and told Lawrence about a new vision he had for Camp Wabanna.

Since the camp had moved to its new location on Likes Road, it had been able to meet all its financial obligations, but there had not been any funds for making improvements. Rev. Emmans shared his vision of starting a Century Club. Each member would contribute $100 a year. In return members would be able to use the camp beach, picnic area, and the campgrounds whenever Camb Wabanna was open.

Lawrence excused himself and called Harriet to verify that there was at least $100 in the checking account. She assured him there was and expressed enthusiasm for being involved in the project! Lawrence and Harriet became the first members of the Century Club. The club grew over the years and was able to help fund many camp projects, coupled with volunteer labor and faithful giving also added may projects – Harmony Hall, a swimming pool, a new snack shop, miniature golf, Key House recreation hall.

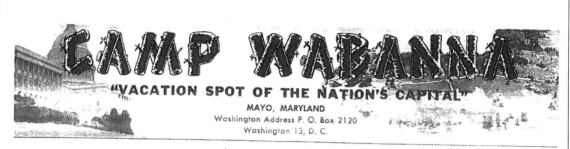

CAMP WABANNA

"VACATION SPOT OF THE NATION'S CAPITAL"

MAYO, MARYLAND
Washington Address P. O. Box 2120
Washington 13, D. C.

Telephones
Winter — 262-2456
262-1181
Summer — 798-0455

October 11, 1966

Dear Wabanna Friend,

As we again bring to your attention Camp Wabanna, it is with real praise and thanksgiving to our heavenly Father for another great year. You will be hearing very shortly details of the summer just ended. Time will not permit me to tell of the many blessings which we received from working with the thousand or more children whom we had this summer during camp weeks at Wabanna. As many of you know, our Bible Conferences were also a rich blessing to all who attended.

Bible Conferences bring rich blessings.

Near the end of the summer construction began on our beautiful new swimming pool. The need for this has been apparent for many years, and a wonderful 35-by-70 foot filtered pool with a 20-by-20 foot diving area will soon be a completed reality. A wading pool for youngsters is also being built. Sea nettles, sea weed, and the increasing pollution of the Bay will no longer be problems.

The pool is a costly operation, yet we feel that a beautiful, completely filtered pool will be a great asset and added attraction for Wabanna. The following is our prayer and plan:

Hundreds enjoy Camp. Many accept Christ as Savior.

First, we are asking all interested in Wabanna to pray with us for the Camp even more definitely than ever before, particularly for the pool.

Second, if you would like to have a part in the pool, your gift, large or small, would be greatly appreciated and we would praise Him exceedingly.

Third, we are putting out a New Bond Issue of $10,000 paying 5 per cent interest. Two dividends are yours in the purchase of bonds--better interest and an investment in the lives of individuals as we are afforded the opportunity of presenting to them our Lord Jesus Christ.

Youth and adults benefit by weekend retreats.

Total cost of the pool is $30,000. We trust that the Lord will lead you to have whatever part you feel led to have. Thanking you for your continued interest, prayer, and support of Wabanna, I remain

Yours in Him,

W. A. Emmans, Director
CAMP WABANNA

THE SPRING OF 1977

In the spring of 1977 camp received some difficult news from the Anne Arundel County Health Department. A letter stated that the camp swimming pool would need a certified lifeguard. In all the prior years, the county only required adult supervision. Camp was in a pickle, as no one was ready and available for this responsibility. There were not many lifeguards in the whole county, and now there was a new demand created by this new law.

Mary Jean stepped up and volunteered to take the rigorous lifeguard training. There was just one catch. She had grown up on a farm and had never really learned how to swim. Float, yes. Swim, no.

When the lifeguard class began, Mary Jean had to learn how to swim. She worked hard, and at one point, did not feel she could ever complete the course. In fact, the only reason she didn't quit was because: "Camp won't be able to open if I don't do this." Mary Jean literally saved the summer!

She was also an expert seamstress. In the early days of camp, the lodge and dorms were furnished with couches and chairs that were donated. These pieces of furniture had been used for many years before they arrived at camp, so they were not in great shape. Most of them had a blanket thrown over them to cover tears and blemishes. Mary Jean removed the old coverings on many of these pieces of furniture and replaced them with new material.

BOB AND MARY FLEMMING: THE BRIDGE OVER TROUBLED WATER

The 1980s presented many difficulties for Camp Wabanna. Reverend Emmans turned eighty in 1982 and was no longer the driving force he once was. He had retired as pastor of First Baptist Church of New Carrollton and the pastor who followed him did not support Camp. In fact, his actions caused some of the church members, who had been supporters of Camp Wabanna, to fall away. Bob Emmans was not well and was not able to do much of anything. Chick Tenley retired as the camp caretaker.

That was when Bob Flemming stepped up. A retired Coast Guard Warrant Officer, Mr. Flemming moved into the caretaker's house and assumed the caretaker's duties.

Bob and his wife, Mary, lived at camp all year round with no other help during the seven month off-season. When camp was open, they were both very much involved in the camp program. Bob worked in the dish room three meals a day, completed repairs to the buildings, and took care of the grass cutting chores. Mary helped clean buildings and they both worked in the arts and crafts program. One year Bob spent the winter making sail boat model kits. In the summer, campers would assemble the kits and race them in the swimming pool. Bob and Mary Flemming were the "Bridge over troubled water."

COUNSELORS, CAMPERS,

WORKERS, WAITRESSES

COUNSELORS

Over the years, Camp Wabanna has been blessed by many young men and women who spend their summer as counselors. Children learn a great deal from the chapel speakers each evening. They also have the opportunity to learn and ask the camp counselors questions during nightly devotions. Just as important, they spend time throughout the day swimming, doing all the activities, and getting to know these Christian young adults.

This experience is rewarding for the camper and the counselor. For most of these young counselors, this is their first taste of ministry. I have often wondered how many of them are now serving in their local churches, as AWANA leaders, Sunday school teachers, deacons, pastors, and even missionaries. I believe it is quite a few.

Diane Schock

Eileen O'Rourke and Ken Decker served as Camp Wabanna counselors before they went to the mission field.

EILEEN O'ROURKE, NURSE AND MISSIONARY, CHINA INLAND MISSION

KEN DECKER, MISSIONARY, SOUTH AMERICA

JEFF

Jeff Clark's first day at camp was not a happy day for him. He was not aware that he was going to be dropped off at Camp Wabanna and would be staying for the entire summer. He wasn't even aware he would be staying for even one night. When he realized that he and his suitcase were being dropped off and he wouldn't be going home for nine weeks, he was really upset. This was not his idea, and I am sure he let everyone at camp know just how upset he was.

The good news is that he met Timmy Leonard, his first friend at camp. Timmy was everyone's first friend at camp. Timmy Leonard also spent the entire summer at camp. He spent every summer at camp from the time he was six until he was sixteen.

Jeff spent many years at camp, and while he wasn't happy at the beginning, he now looks back fifty years and talks about how important those years at Camp Wabanna were to him. He heard the Bible preached in chapel and talked about the Bible in devotions in the cabin at night. I talked to Jeff recently. He is now sixty years and. He loves the Lord and the memories he has of Camp Wabanna.

TIMMY

I don't believe anyone spent more nights as a camper at Camp Wabanna than Timmy. He told me John White led him to the Lord very early in his time at camp and he has never doubted his salvation. Timmy has been a friend of the Teuling family since the early 1960s and is still in touch with them even today.

What I don't know is how he survived so many nights in the worker's cabin. The worker's cabin wasn't much bigger than a closet. It was on the back of the Three Flats. The ceiling had zero insulation and there was hardly any air circulation. Some nights that room would never cool down. There would be five or six teenage boys trying to get some sleep on those hot summer nights. Timmy did that all summer, every night for several years; I don't know how he did it. He also sat through the movie *Old Yeller* more than anyone on so many rainy days over the years.

DONNA

Donna was packed and ready to go to camp two weeks before camp started. She returned to camp in 2020. Donna recounted how, in the 1980s, she and her mom were living with her grandfather, Norman Green. He helped build Harmony Hall when he was a teenager.

Norman wanted Donna to learn the truth about God's plan of salvation through Jesus Christ. To learn that Jesus was everything He said He was, and promised us a place in God's eternal family if we put our faith and trust in Him.

Mr. Green made sure she was involved in Sunday school and AWANA at First Baptist Church of New Carrollton. Donna also spent many weeks at Camp Wabanna over several years. She was a terrific swimmer, and at eight years old she easily beat other campers in the Saturday swim races. She even beat boys and girls six years older than she was.

During her walk around the camp, after being away for thirty years, she reflected on how much camp meant to her as a child.

EARLY YEARS ACTIVITIES

Camp activities in 50s, 60s, 70s, and 80s were very basic. We played a lot of kickball, volleyball, and softball with antiquated equipment. We had heavy, hard to maneuver row boats, and an old fire engine to climb on. We had three swings, which were so popular you had to wait around for a turn and hope someone would get off before the bell rang. There were three ponies—Charlie, Pepsi, and I can't remember the other one's name. The younger children really liked to ride the ponies, and the older campers liked to pet them and feed them apples. Because they were only used six weeks out of the year, the cost of feeding them and the veterinary bills made them cost prohibitive. They had to be discontinued from the camp program.

In the evenings we had scavenger hunts, tug of war, and hikes around the neighborhood. For a while the youngest campers played a game called Red Rover, which had to be discontinued when we realized that more campers were showing up in the nurse's office after playing Red Rover than any other activity.

For a while we had the Camp Wabanna 'W', which was just a wooden letter. Every day one of us would hide the 'W' somewhere on the camp grounds and the camper who found it could turn it in for a snack. It was very popular with the young campers. We also had a mini golf course for a short while, but being made of wood, it was no match for the Chesapeake Bay winters.

STACY TAYLOR RIDING PEPSI

FRANK

One of the most labor intensive aspects of a summer camp is that everyone has to eat. Three times a day the kitchen crew has to step up and keep the nourishment flowing. During the 70s and 80s we had a retired Marine cook named Frank. He was really great. He would go to sleep really early so that he could get up early and get breakfast ready when the campers showed up. Frank loved camp, he loved the kids, and he loved being part of it. When he was at camp, he was very involved. He had his own opinions about things, which sometimes were good, and sometimes weren't.

In order to provide all these meals for everyone, Frank needed the help of teenage guys and gals. These young people worked hard and were the stars of the show at meal time. The counselor would raise his or her hand, and within minutes, more pancakes or potatoes or salad would be rushed to the table. They cleaned up and cleaned the dishes and the tables, and then reset for the next meal.

Between meals they would assist with other camp projects. They did all this for $7.00 a week – yes, $1.00 a day! For the most part, they all were glad to be part of camp's mission.

One year Rocky Williams was at Camp Wabanna as a worker. He washed dishes three times a day, and between meals he helped dig a huge hole for a septic tank. It was hot and he would purchase cold Pepsi and Fresca. He agreed to pay for these soft drinks when he got paid at the end of the week. When he got paid his $7.00, he went to the shack shop to pay his bill. He was told he owed $10.00 and he paid his bill!

DAVE HATTENFIELD, STACY TAYLOR, ANGIE THOMAS

PRANKS

Over the years, many pranks have been played on camp counselors, campers, and the staff. The goal is to make sure that the pranks are safe and don't cause any bad feelings. One October night the snack shop was in full swing; the view of the fall harvest moon on the Chesapeake Bay was amazing. Many retreat attendees walked out to the seawall to take it all in. They did not know that Doug had draped himself with seaweed and hidden just out of view at the bottom of the sea wall. At just the right time he climbed to the top of the wall growing and covered with seaweed. He had a flashlight showing his face wearing a monster mask. He scared a few people that night, however, it was all in good fun.

One summer day, just before the campers came into the dining room, Connie, a waitress that summer, filled all the glasses at her two tables with Kool-Aid…all the way to the top, 100% full! The glasses were so full that you wouldn't dare pick up the glass for fear of spilling the Kool-Aid. We could not even pull out the chairs to sit down for fear of spilling it. We finally figured out we needed to bend over the chair and take a sip before we pulled out the chair.

THREE FLATS

HARMONY HALL

VOLUNTEERS

During the early years, volunteers played an enormous role in the operation and improvements of Camp Wabanna.

One of the most unusual projects that we had a part in came in the summer of 1969. Reverend Emmans announced from the pulpit that someone had given a house to camp. The plan was to get a company to take it off the foundation and move it intact to Likes Road. However, the house was too tall to go down the street without interfering with electrical wires and tree branches. Plan B was to ask the men of the church to take the house down board by board and rebuilt it at camp.

I remember being allowed to slam my foot into the wall and tear the plaster away from the boards. I also remember being on top of the house. I had a crowbar and would pry one end of each board loose. Bob Owen would be on the other end doing the same thing. Then we would drop the board down to the ground and put it on the truck.

The people who gave us the house thought we were not going fast enough. They wanted the house out of their way. Their project was to build a shopping center on that spot (near East Pines in Riverdale, Maryland). Bob Hall had a great idea! He got out his chain saw and cut the walls into sections that could fit into the truck. Rebuilding the house was like putting together a giant jigsaw puzzle. I remember Charlie Harvey putting the front porch together; it was quite a challenge.

JUSTIN TAYLOR, CHARLIE HARVEY

When I was about thirteen, Reverend Emmans called our house. My mom called me to the phone. He asked what I was doing that day, and I said I wasn't doing anything. He replied that he'd be right by to pick me up. We were going to the Pentagon.

I didn't know why we were going to the Pentagon, but when we got there we were allowed to go into the loading area. Reverend Emmans had procured wooden chairs for Camp Wabanna and First Baptist Church of Carrollton. They were fifty cents each and we had two trucks. We loaded those trucks so high that the top of the load wobbled back and forth and had to be tied down. We stacked them so high we couldn't get out the door, so we had to unload the top of both trucks and restack them on the other side of the exit. All through Washington DC we had to be careful that we didn't hit any low-lying trees or electrical wires. We got enough chairs to fill the dining hall at camp as well as the basement, which was being used for the sanctuary of First Baptist Church at the time. That was the first time I'd been called to work as a volunteer for camp.

MUSICIANS AND CAMP EVANGELISTS

———— ◆ ————

THE PHILLIPS FAMILY

Homer (1912 – 1974) and Blanch Phillips (1916 – 1998) had amazing musical talents. During the 1940s, 1950s, and 1960s, they, along with their two sons Doug and Bob, were very involved with in the church musical ministry of Maryland Avenue Baptist Church and Landover Hills Baptist Church. It didn't stop there, however, because as a family, they were committed to the spread of the Gospel. They received and accepted invitations to minister in many other Bible conferences, missionary conferences, and revival meetings. Oftentimes they would drive many miles back and forth for several nights during the work week in support of other church's conferences. It was not unusual for them to drive an hour or two each way.

I don't remember my Dad on the board but I do know our family talked about Camp (Wabanna) quite a bit. We did spend much time at Wabanna providing music. I vividly remember practicing my trumpet in my room there overlooking the "Sea Wall" with lots of people enjoying the grounds.
Also, I remember the very best and well known Bible teachers and evangelists every week as featured guests! Really, it was a "Who's-Who" of the evangelical world! I now see that was a rare life experience.

*I also want to give you some information on Glenn Wagner. Wagner played
football at the University of Illinois; he was a big lineman. He came to Washington
DC and became the president of the Washington Bible College. I think he was
the first president and was very close with my mom and dad musically.
I went to Argentina with his son Glenn, Jr. one summer along with the
Pocket Testament League. Wagner was a great influence on my life.*
— Doug Phillips
Jer. 33:3

HOMER, BLANCHE, ROBERT, AND DOUG PHILLIPS

The Phillips Family and Wabanna

The year was 1939 and a young trombone soloist was being featured on a concert band performance in Grant Park, downtown Chicago. Little did he know that the concert being broadcast nationally on radio was being heard by the director of the United States Navy Band, Washington D.C. This professional concert band, known as the "World's Finest", was searching for a new trombone soloist. After a final audition in the Nation's Capital, Homer Phillips along with his new wife, Blanche, packed their bags and moved to the Maryland suburbs of Washington. Blanche had her own professional credentials as a concert pianist and a featured soloist in an opera company located in Chicago.

Before long, Blanche was hired as a soprano soloist by Metropolitan Baptist Church, just several blocks from the Nation's Capitol Building. In time, this same church was looking for a Minister of Music and Homer accepted the call to this ministry position. During WW 2, Homer and Blanche Phillips became close friends with Glenn and Lucretia Wagner. Rev. Wagner was an All-American football player at the University of Illinois. When he received Christ as Savior, he went to seminary and felt God's call to become a missionary. Rev. Wagner started a ministry reaching military members passing through Washington during the war years and convinced Homer and Blanche to join the ministry at a Service Members Center and on a Christian radio broadcast. Later, Glenn became the President of the Washington Bible College and convinced the Phillips' to join the faculty. Glenn Wagner continued his storied ministry as Foreign Field Secretary for the Pocket Testament League.

The late 1940's and early 50's was a time before television was a ubiquitous item in every American home, and most homes and churches did not have air conditioning. Bible conference centers became popular for their great Christian speakers, music, and beautiful get-away locations out and away from steamy cities. Some of these included "Camp of the Woods" and "Word of Life Camp", both in the Adirondack Mountains of New York. But the mountains of New York were a little far for the residents of Washington, Baltimore and Annapolis. Thus, Camp Wabanna was born. Homer Phillips became a member of the Board of Directors of Wabanna. Thus began a period when Homer and Blanche provided worship music at the camp. Their two sons, Doug and Bob became brass players like their dad, and joined the family evangelistic music team as they reached their pre-teen years.

The meetings at Wabanna were well attended with wonderful speakers like Ding Touiling, and Dr. Ralph Keiper. Dr Keiper was a research assistant for the famous Bible teacher, pastor and theologian, Donald Barnhouse. Dr. Keiper went on to gain a national reputation as a Bible teacher, writer and seminary professor. While he had several handicaps (being blind in one eye and legally blind in the other), he was able to read from the Bible with a magnifying glass. That in no way diminished the brilliant teacher expounding upon the Word with a delightful mix of humor and incredible insight into the text's meaning and application. Glenn Wagner continued with Pocket Testament League for years; but when he was not overseas, he came back to the states and on occasion, also spoke at Wabanna.

And we should never forget another speaker at the Bible Conference, Rev. William Emmons. While he was an outstanding preacher with a wonderful command of the entire Bible, he loved preaching from Romans and Revelation. It was under his pastoral leadership of Maryland Avenue Baptist Church in Washington, D.C that the church moved to a new location in the Maryland suburbs, a church which became First Baptist Church, New Carrollton, Maryland. During the early years while at Maryland Avenue Baptist, the Lord gave him a vision for the Wabanna Bible Conference on the Chesapeake Bay in Maryland. It was Pastor Emmons' vision and driving force which God used to create Wabanna, which continues to host Bible conferences which teach, enrich, and evangelize
participants to this day!

Robert Phillips

GLENN WAGNER (1907 - 1977)

Mr. Wagner played a huge part in post-war Japan. General Douglas MacArthur, after taking charge of Japan, asked for Christian organizations to come to minister to the war torn Japanese people.

Mitsuo Fuchida was the commander of the air attack on Pearl Harbor. After the war he joined the Pocket Testament League. He spent the rest of his life serving Jesus Christ as a member of the PTL (Pocket Testament League). The PTL gave out over eight million copies of the Gospel of John in post-war Japan. The Phillips family and Glenn Wagner worked together in many local Bible conferences in the DC area and at Camp Wabanna.

Glenn Wagner was the first president of the Washington Bible College. Reverend Emmans taught classes at Washington Bible College in the 1940s and 1950s. For nearly forty years, Camp Wabanna gave a copy of the Gospel of John to each and every camper. They were encouraged to take it home and reach one chapter every day. I have to believe that was an extension of the PTL from Glenn Wagner to Reverend Emmans to Camp Wabanna. Please take time to visit Pocket Testament League's Virtual Museum at https://ht.ptl.org. The PTL was endorsed by General MacArthur, President Eisenhower, and President Kennedy. General MacArthur requested that the PTL provide ten million copies of the Gospel of John to distribute throughout Japan following the end of the war. League members and supporters responded graciously, with eleven million Gospels actually distributed. On December 8, 1949 MacArthur provided this letter of support to The Pocket Testament League.

General Douglas MacArthur requested that the League provide 10 million Testaments to distribute throughout Japan following the end of the war. League members and supporters responded graciously, with 11 million Gospels actually distributed. On December 8, 1949 MacArthur provided this letter of support to The Pocket Testament League.

**GENERAL HEADQUARTERS
SUPREME COMMANDER FOR THE ALLIED POWERS**
OFFICE OF THE SUPREME COMMANDER

8 December 1949.

Dear Doctor Kunz:

I have received with greatest interest the report of yourself, Glenn W. Wagner and Edwin L. Frizen, representatives of the Pocket Testament League, including letters of grateful appreciation addressed to the League by presidents of the leading universities of Japan.

The magnificent and constructive work which the League is doing for the Japanese Nation has my hearty endorsement. This demonstration of practical Christianity is making a vital contribution toward meeting the heart needs of this people by means of mass meetings with wide distribution of the Scriptures, which reveal the knowledge of God and His love through Jesus Christ.

I sincerely trust that the people of America will grasp the present opportunity afforded by a merciful God to lay the foundation for a true and living faith, and I urgently request that Christian people everywhere shall support the Pocket Testament League in their noble efforts to meet the challenge of this crucial hour.

With cordial regard.

Very faithfully,

DOUGLAS MacARTHUR

Dr. Alfred A. Kunz, Executive Director,
The Pocket Testament League, Inc.,
156 Fifth Avenue,
New York 10, New York.

On July 11, 1953 President Dwight D. Eisenhower penned this letter in support of the work of the league. Printed on White House Stationery, it reads:

On July 11, 1953 US president Dwight D. Eisenhower penned this letter in support of the work of the League. Printed on White House stationery, it reads:

July 11, 1953

Man's dignity and freedom, the cornerstone of our structure of free government, have their source and substance in deeply felt religion. In the highest sense the Bible is to us the unique repository of eternal spiritual truths. In the most tangible sense, it is the ultimate and indispensable source of inspiration for America's life in freedom. By enabling men to renew, in their minds and spirits, the religious concepts of equality, justice and mercy, the Pocket Testament League, and all others engaged in distributing the Bible, have dedicated themselves to a noble work.

Signed, Dwight D. Eisenhower

THE WHITE HOUSE
WASHINGTON

July 11, 1953.

Man's dignity and freedom, the cornerstone of our structure of free government, have their source and substance in deeply felt religion. In the highest sense the Bible is to us the unique repository of eternal spiritual truths. In the most tangible sense, it is the ultimate and indispensable source of inspiration for America's life in freedom. By enabling men to renew, in their minds and spirits, the religious concepts of equality, justice and mercy, the Pocket Testament League, and all others engaged in distributing the Bible, have dedicated themselves to a noble work.

Dwight Eisenhower

On November 20, 1961, President John F. Kennedy penned this letter in support of the work of the league. Printed on White House Stationery, it reads:

On November 20, 1961 US president John F. Kennedy penned this letter in support of the work of the League. Printed on White House stationery, it reads:

November 20, 1961

The Bible is the common heritage of all men. It is the foundation upon which the great democratic traditions and institutions of our country stand. Recognizing what it has meant to the development of our American way of life, we can hope that other nations and societies will also find light and guidance in this book.

It is good to learn of the campaigns through which the Pocket Testament League has distributed more than 20 million Scripture portions in Japan, Korea, Formosa, Southeast Asia, Europe, to our Armed Forces during the two World Wars and the Korean War, and more recently in the emerging nations of Africa.

As you embark on a continent-wide effort in South America, I want to extend my sincere wishes for your success in this timely distribution of the Word of God.

Sincerely, John Kennedy

THE WHITE HOUSE

WASHINGTON

November 20, 1961

Dear Mr. Kunz:

The Bible is the common heritage of all men. It is the foundation upon which the great democratic traditions and institutions of our country stand. Recognizing what it has meant to the development of our American way of life, we can hope that other nations and societies will also find light and guidance in this book.

It is good to learn of the campaigns through which the Pocket Testament League has distributed more than 20 million Scripture portions in Japan, Korea, Formosa, Southeast Asia, Europe, to our Armed Forces during the two World Wars and the Korean War, and more recently in the emerging nations of Africa.

As you embark on a continent-wide effort in South America, I want to extend my sincere wishes for your success in this timely distribution of the Word of God.

Sincerely,

John Kennedy

Mr. Alfred A. Kunz
International Director
The Pocket Testament League
49 Honeck Street
Englewood, New Jersey

REVEREND DINGEMAN (1918 - 2016) AND GLORIA (1924 - 2015) TEULING

Camp Wabanna was founded as a Christian camp for children, and also to be a home for Bible conferences. During the 1950s, 60s, 70s, and 80s, many traveling evangelists visited camp each summer. Reverend Ding Teuling and his family came for a week of meeting *every year for thirty six years.*

Reverend Teuling was unique in that after he presented his evening message he would draw a picture using a special chalk. When he turned a special black light on the picture, a second picture would appear. Both pictures would serve as an illustration of the message he had presented. Everyone was impressed with his Bible knowledge and his artistic talent.

Ding Teuling, founder of Teuling Enterprises, was born April 23, 1918, in Muskegon, Michigan, He was inspired as a young man by chalk artists like Esther Frye, and the first black light chalk artist, Karl Steele. Ding perfected his fine art abilities as a commercial artist and as he presented his black light chalk art programs before youth groups and churches.

When he married, he and his family continued his traveling evangelistic chalk art ministry together. The impact of Ding's outstanding preaching, Gloria's amazing piano playing and music multiplied the effectiveness of his Bible illustrations. Even small churches had record crowds with standing room only. Some churches even had huge overflow crowds watching through the church windows and doors. Revivals broke out reaching such a multitude of people that his meetings had to be extended.

Ding and Gloria Teuling

From 1937, Ding and Gloria not only inspired the congregations in many churches in the US and foreign countries, but they also inspired missionaries, pastors, evangelists and keynote speakers to dedicate their gifts and talents minister through chalk art. Some of these 'students' include Bill Gothard, Rod Snow, Matt Bowman, Peggy Esher and his own son Dave Teuling. For over 50 years, thousands of chalk art students have benefited from Ding's classes, workshops and training materials.

Ding Teuling's Chalk Art Classes and Workshops

Ding's presentations are still remembered today as the best experience ever, in some of the world's finest churches. Ding is still recognized throughout the world as one of the leading pioneers of black-light drawing. He is known as the Dean of chalk art. Many of His students are leaders in the field of Chalk Art today.

Through the years, he designed his own one-of-a-kind easel, utilizing the best technology available. His lighting system included two mercury vapor black lights with an electronic trap-door, along with three fluorescent tube-type black lights. He designed swivel light mounts for his colored bulbs and used a single adjustable spotlight that was dimmed to reveal his black light pictures.

When Ding began to manufacture his own black light chalk, he perfected his formulae for each color as skillfully as he did everything else in his life. His hand-crafted, artist-quality went into every stick of chalk.

He picked up his first stick of chalk and began his drawing over 70 years ago. We not only marveled at his brilliant mastery of each detail, but we also were touched that he was willing to share his mastery from an open heart with all who would love to learn.

But we only witnessed a very small part of his genius…Because it was not until Saturday, September 3 at 7:25 PM, at 98 years old, that God flipped on His black-light! What a miraculous, astonishing and amazing hidden picture must have been crafted. It all remains to be seen, when the angels gather his chalks and papers to form the beautiful mosaic that was the life and artwork of Ding Teuling. -Dan Ondra

Teuling Enterprises. Inc... (231) 798-2444....... chalklady@juno.com

LESTER AND GRACE PLACE

Lester and Grace Place also came for many summers. They were unique in that they led the worship service using many different instruments: the marimba, the xylophone, the triple octave chime, the guitar, and many other instruments. Grace and Lester would play their instruments, and then Lester would bring a gospel message. They traveled all over the country as well as to many provinces in Canada. It was a real treat to be at camp and participate in all the activities during the day, and then be able to hear these men, as well as others, bring gospel messages at the end of the day.

My good friend Craig Moore has a unique perspective on Camp Wabanna. He can relate to us based on his experiences as a Camp Wabanna camper, worker, counselor, project volunteer, and evangelist.

MY EXPERIENCES AT CAMP WABANNA

CRAIG MOORE

MY FIRST EXPERIENCE AT CAMP WAS WHEN I WAS A CAMPER THERE IN 1956, AS AN 8-YEAR-OLD FROM THE BAPTIST HOME FOR CHILDREN, WHERE I SPENT A YEAR. THE SNACK SHOP WAS OVER BY THE FARMHOUSE AND WE SWAM IN THE BAY.

IN 1964 MY MOTHER SENT ME TO CAMP AS A WORKER FOR THE SUMMER. I WAS 16 AT THE TIME. I HELPED BOB EMMANS BUILD AND INSTALL NEW SEA NETTLE NETS AND GET A NEW DIVING BOARD (A REGULAR LARGE PLANK OF WOOD), TO REPLACE THE ONE WHICH HAD BEEN BROKEN. I REMEMBER BOB EMMANS WITNESSING TO CAMPERS MANY TIMES, AND I LOVED IT WHEN HE QUOTED FROM MEMORY HIS FAVORITE POEM, "THE TOUCH OF THE MASTERS HAND".

I WAS PLACED IN THE FRONT ROOM OF THE "CLEF" TO HELP HARRY GRIFFIN, THE COUNSELOR THERE, WITH 12-14 YEAR OLD BOYS. I WAS TOUCHED BY HARRY'S LIFE AND THAT SUMMER ACCEPTED CHRIST AS MY SAVIOR THROUGH HIS DEVOTIONS AT NIGHT. WORKERS DID JUST ABOUT EVERYTHING AT CAMP: KITCHEN DUTY, TRIPS TO BALTIMORE TO GET FREE PEANUT BUTTER, RAISINS, ETC., AND SUPPLIES. I WAS ALSO RESPONSIBLE FOR RUNNING THE OLD "REEL" MOVIES AFTER EACH SWIM IN THE AFTERNOON. WE REALLY WORE OUT THOSE FREE "TRAVEL" PRESENTATIONS; WHEN THE

1

MOVIE PROJECTOR WASN'T "EATING" THE FILM AND HAD TO BE CORRECTED.

I LEARNED A LOT AND ENJOYED THE WORK. DURING THE OFF-SEASON I WENT TO CAMP TO DO JOBS THAT WERE NEEDED; CARRYING CEMENT, ONE BUCKET AT A TIME, DOWN TO THE FRONT WALL FOR REV. EMMANS TO LAY THE BRICK; HELPING BUILD THE THREE FLATS AND OTHER BUILDINGS. I REMEMBER HELPING IN THE KITCHEN ONE WEEKEND WITH LARRY FRYE. WE HAD TO SLEEP IN THE CLEF WITH NO HEAT, TEMPERATURES BELOW FREEZING, AND STACKED A HALF DOZEN QUILTS ON US TO SURVIVE THE NIGHT. IN THOSE YEARS THERE WAS NO HEAT OR AIR-CONTIONING IN THE CABINS, SO WE WOULD JUST SWEAT OURSELVES TO SLEEP AND DID FINE.

IN 1965 I CAME BACK AS A COUNSELOR, WHICH I DID FOR SEVERAL YEARS IN A ROW. THOSE EXPERIENCES WERE VERY SPECIAL. I LOVED THE BEDTIME DEVOTIONS AND THE SIMPLE BUT SINCERE PRAYERS OF THE KIDS EXPREESSING THEIR THOUGHTS TO THE LORD. I ALSO LOVED THE SPECIAL WEEKS WHEN REV. DING TUELING CAME AND MINISTERED WITH CHALKART USING BLACK LIGHTS. THIS MINISTRY TOUCHED MANY PEOPLE'S HEARTS AND MOTIVATED ME TO TAKE CLASSES FROM DING AND BEGIN DRAWING PICTURES MYSELF. I REMEMBER MANY EVENINGS DRAWING PICTURES, SINGING DUETS WITH TRACI KING (WARNICK), AND MINISTERING TO THE KIDS. OVER THE YEARS I DREW

2

CLOSE TO FIFTY PICTURES AT THE CAMP. I ALSO LOVED THE MINISTRY OF LESTER AND GRACE PLACE AND THE MANY SERMONS BY DR. ANDREW TELFORD. THE LAST TIME I DREW A PICTURE AT CAMP, IN THE EARLY 2000S, A YOUNG MAN NAMED NEAL LUEBBERS WAS MINISTERING THERE, AND LATER BECAME, AND IS CURRENTLY, THE DIRECTOR OF THE CAMP.

AFTER A FEW YEARS THE CAMP INSTALLED A NEW SWIMMING POOL, AND WAKING UP WITH SAND IN OUR SHEETS, AND OTHER PLACES, ENDED. NO MORE SEA NETTLE STINGS OR STEPPING ON HORSE-SHOE CRABS. I ENJOYED THE ROW BOATS AND MANY ACTIVITIES THAT THE KIDS ENJOYED AND SHOWED THEM THAT CHRISTIANS CAN HAVE FUN ALSO, HOWEVER, SOMETIMES IT COULD BE DANGEROUS; I REMEMBER WHILE TEACHING ARCHERY, A YOUNG BOY SHOT AN ARROW WAY TO HIGH AND IT STUCK IN THE BACK OF THE CLEF! THANK THE LORD, NO ONE WAS HURT.

I REMEMBER SOME OF THE SPECIAL OLDER WORKERS AND VOLUNTEERS AT CAMP. FRANK AND PAUL, THE COOKS, JIMMY RYMAN MOWING THE LAWN, CHARLIE EDGE HELPING WITH ANY JOB, CHARLEY HARVEY, REMO MOSCATELLI, AND BOB FLEMING.

OVER THE YEARS MARYLAND AVENUE BAPTIST CHURCH AND NEW CARROLLTON BAPTIST CHURCH PLAYED A HUGE ROLE AT CAMP WABANNA, BEING THE HOME CHURCHS OF THE EMMAN'S FAMILY. IT SHOWS HOW

CRITICAL IT IS FOR LOCAL CHURCHES TO SUPPORT THE MINISTRY OF CAMP WABANNA.

AROUND 1969 A LOT OF THE COUNSELORS WERE FROM WASHINGTON BIBLE COLLEGE, AND THROUGH THEIR TESTIMONY I BEGAN ATTENDING WBC AND GRADUATED IN 1972.

I REMEMBER CERTAIN CAMPERS WHO STOOD OUT, SUCH AS DALE PRUITT, WHO ATE SO MANY PANCAKES HE BECAME KNOW AS "DALE PANCAKE PRUITT". TIMMY LEONARD, WHO HAD RUBBER BANDS IN HIS TEETH FOR BRACES, AND FINDING LITTLE RUBBER BANDS EVERYWHERE. ALSO, JEFF CLARK, WHO WAS A CHALLENGE AT TIMES, BUT I BELIEVE WAS SINCERELY AFFECTED BY THE CAMP. I ALSO REMEMBER BOB EMMANS ALLOWING LARRY FRYE AND ME TO GO BACK UP HOME TO PLAY FOR THE NEW CARROLLTON SOFTBALL TEAM.

SUNDAY DINNERS WERE ALWAYS A GREAT MEAL WITH ROAST BEEF, MASH POTATOES WITH GRAVY, AND PEAS. YOUNG PEOPLE FROM THE BAPTIST HOME WERE SPECIAL

4

TO ME ALSO, I KNEW FROM EXPERIENCE WHAT THEY WERE DEALING WITH. AND CAMP GAVE MANY OF THEM A HOPE IN CHRIST, THAT THEY NEVER HAD, JUST AS IT DID FOR ME. I ALSO REMEMBER DAILY CABIN INSPECTION REPORTS BY MARY ELLEN RYMAN, WHEN CERTAIN BOYS WERE EXPOSED FOR STUFFING WET, SANDY, BATHING SUITS, INTO THEIR DRESSER DRAWERS TO APPEAR TO HAVE A CLEAN CABIN. I REMEMBER WEEKEND RETREATS WITH THE YOUNG PEOPLE FROM NEW CARROLLTON BAPTIST CHURCH. REMO MOSCATELLI AND I USE TO SEE HOW FAR WE COULD SWIM UNDER WATER IN THE POOL.

I RETURNED TO CAMP FOR THE 75TH ANNIVERSARY WHERE DING AND GLORIA TUELING WERE PRESENT AND GOT TO SEE MANY OLD FRIENDS AND SHARE MANY FOND MEMORIES OF CAMP.

THE LORD HAS USED THE MINISTRY OF CAMP WABANNA FOR MANY YEARS TO LEAD MANY KIDS TO A SAVING KNOWLEDGE OF CHRIST AND GROW IN THEIR CHRISTIAN WALK. TODAY, THE CAMP IS AS VIBRANT AS EVER, AND STILL HAS A MAJOR IMPACT ON MANY YOUNG PEOPLE FOR THE LORD.

IN CHRIST,

CRAIG MOORE

THE TOUCH OF THE MASTER'S HAND

'Twas battered and scarred,
And the auctioneer thought it
hardly worth his while
To waste his time on the old violin,
but he held it up with a smile.
"What am I bid, good people", he cried,
"Who starts the bidding for me?"
"One dollar, one dollar, Do I hear two?"
"Two dollars, who makes it three?"
"Three dollars once, three dollars twice, going for three,"
But, No,
From the room far back a gray bearded man
Came forward and picked up the bow,
Then wiping the dust from the old violin
And tightening up the strings,
He played a melody, pure and sweet
As sweet as the angel sings.
The music ceased and the auctioneer
With a voice that was quiet and low,
Said "What now am I bid for this old violin?"
As he held it aloft with its' bow.
"One thousand, one thousand, Do I hear
two?" "Two thousand, Who makes it three?"
"Three thousand once, three thousand
twice, Going and gone", said he.
The audience cheered,
But some of them cried,
"We just don't understand."
"What changed its' worth?"
Swift came the reply.

"The Touch of the Masters Hand."
"And many a man with life out of tune
All battered and bruised with hardship
Is auctioned cheap to a thoughtless crowd
Much like that old violin
A mess of pottage, a glass of wine,
A game and he travels on.
He is going once, he is going twice,
He is going and almost gone.
But the Master comes,
And the foolish crowd never can quite understand,
The worth of a soul and the change that is wrought
By the Touch of the Masters' Hand.
- Myra Brooks Welch

THE CHESAPEAKE PAVILION

As you drive in the front gate of Camp Wabanna, you are driving toward the Chesapeake Pavilion. The Chesapeake Pavilion is dedicated to the memory of Thawley Holmes and his wife Virginia.

Everett and Connie Yates Golihew both spent time at Camp Wabanna as campers and counselors. They both have fond memories of their wonderful friends at Maryland Avenue Baptist Church. Everett and Connie now have grandchildren spending time at Camp Wabanna as campers, making them fourth generation family members to have a role in Camp Wabanna.

Everett's Aunt Elizabeth was the church secretary for Maryland Avenue Baptist Church and was so good at keeping the church organized and operating during the week that Reverend Emmons was able to put extra time in at the camp.

Connie's parents were wonderful members of Maryland Avenue Baptist and supporters of Camp Wabanna and the N.E. Mission.

My first recollection of Connie's father, Mr. Harry Yates, was at Griffith Stadium. My parents took me to see the Washington Senators play in the mid 1950s. We ran into Mr. Yates at the front gate. During the fourth inning he came to where we were sitting. He had purchased a baseball souvenir pin for me, which I immediately attached to my shirt. I was perhaps seven or eight years old. It was a big deal for me and now, sixty five years later, I still remember my friend Mr. Yates doing that for me. I also remember the score of the game: Washington Senators 4, Cleveland 2. After that game I would seek out Mr. Yates at church functions to talk baseball.

Everett and Connie have also been supporters of Thawley Holmes and his work over the years. I asked Everett and Connie to share with us about Thawley and Virginia, and their ministries.

THAWLEY (1904 - 1984) AND VIRGINIA (1907 - 1993) HOLMES

The idea of a Rescue Mission in northeast Washington DC was first envisioned by Reverend Emmans of Maryland Avenue Baptist Church. Plans were made in 1936. A mission began in the 1300 block of H Street, northeast. Thawley Holmes, an insurance agent, felt led by the Lord to resign from his job and work full time as a director of the mission. Supported by churches and individuals of different denominations, the mission cared for transient men. He fed the hungry and provided beds for the weary, but his main interest was to reach these men with the gospel.

After World War II a survey was taken in Rockville, Maryland, revealing that a community church was needed. Men from the Northeast Rescue Mission built the Pines Community Church. Mr. Holmes was ordained and pastored the church from 1946 until 1964. In 1949 the mission moved to 8ᵗʰ Street, northeast, where Reverend Holmes ministered until he died in 1984.

In 1985 the Board of Trustees of the mission invited the central Union Mission to operate Holmes House. It operated as a home for battered and abused women.

--Everett Golihew

Maryland Avenue Baptist also fielded a men's fast pitch softball team. Mr. Yates' son Steve played third base.

Eugene Stark Pitcher
Mel Matthews Catcher
Bob Andrews 1st base
Everett Golihew 2nd base
West Swim Short stop
Steve Yates 3rd base
Buster Teague Left field
Ronnie Benoit Center field
Butch Bryant Right field
Larry Frye Bench

Now why would I put this list of players on a softball team in a Camp Wabanna book? The reason is that one of my key points of emphasis is how the good folks of Maryland Avenue Baptist Church were a family. Everyone on this list played softball together, worshipped together, worked at Camp Wabanna together and supported the N.E. Mission. We were one together church!

In writing *Camp Wabanna: The Early Years*, I have only been able to introduce you to a precious few people who are part of the camp story. There are thousands of stories about campers who were introduced to God's love for them; stories of counselors; stories of those who have either time, money, or both to camp; stories of fun filled days and spiritual victories won; and stories about friendships, long term and short term.

If you have a story, please send it to:

Camp Wabanna
101 Likes Road
Edgewater, MD 21037
Attention: Camp History.

If you are currently involved in camp, may God bless you! You are still writing your story. We are so very anxious to hear each and every story. We have eternity to get to hear from everyone.

Give praise to the Lord, proclaim his name among
the nations what he has done!
1 Chronicles 16:8

ACKNOWLEDGEMENTS

I felt led to write *Camp Wabanna: The Early Years* because I wanted everyone to know about the folks who were here in the beginning. I know I speak for them when I say that if you are currently involved with the camp, YOU are our hero. Everyone who has a part, big or small, the work you do is so very important

I would like to thank everyone who helped me put *Camp Wabanna: The Early Years* together. Thank you to Everett, Craig, Remo, Buddy, and David Teuling for the articles you submitted. Thank you to Beth for the many hours you put into researching the camp timeline (found on the next three pages). Using the timeline, I just had to add in the personalities.

I would like to thank Shannon and Tara for their help when I needed it in the camp office. I would also like to thank my daughter, Stacy Taylor, for her good advice and help when I would come to a computer road block that I couldn't figure out.

Thank you, Sherry Wynne Tucker, for helping me get to the finish line. I was floundering as I got to the end of this process and you volunteered to give me some pointers. I needed much more help than just pointers. Thank you for everything you did.

HISTORICAL TIMELINE

THE PRODUCT OF MANY YEARS OF DIGGING INTO THE DETAILS

BY BETH HOLM

Collaborative History   People   Camp History   Land History

Decade	Year/ Date	Event
1850 - 1860		
	1857	Thomas E. Collison is born; he is who owned the land prior to the Likes family
	1859	Fred Steiner is born to Ann and Frederick Steiner who is a carriage maker by trade in Frederick City
1860 - 1870		
	December 7th, 1870	Sylvan H. Likes is born
1870 - 1880		
	1878	Mamie B. Likes is born
1880 - 1890		
	July 2nd, 1884	Sylvan H. Likes passed public school exam and is accepted into City College
	June 26th, 1889	Sylvan returned home after traveling abroad for one year for the advanced study of medicine
1890 - 1900		
	September 30th, 1899	Dr. Sylvan H. Likes and his mother, Mrs. Henry Likes returned from a trip abroad to study hostpitals and for his he
1900 - 1910		
	November 29th, 1902	William A. Emmans is born
	Sunday, March 05, 1905	Maryland Avenue Baptist Church is founded
1910 - 1920		
	July 1st, 1910	Sylvan H. Likes purchases about 30 acres on the Chesapeake Bay from Thomas E. Collison
	Sunday, May 07, 1911	Sylvan H. Likes purchases 1/2 interest in a yacht from Albert H. Likes for $5 named "Old Glory" (Baltimore Sun)
	Wednesday, October 18th, 1911	Sylvan H. Likes (age 40) marries Mamie B. Leopold (age 32) at his mother Lina's house residence by Rabbi Dr. C. Rubenstein; only immediate family were there
	February 25th, 1912	Dr. Sylvan H. Likes, with listed address of 1610 Eutaw Place (his mother's address) purchases a 30 horsepower ro:
	August 4th, 1914	Mamie Likes gives birth to OR ADOPTS son David Henry Levy Likes (1914 - 1986)
	January 30th, 1920	Anne Arundel County Census Bureau lists Thomas E. Collison as a farmer, age 63 and his wife Mary E. also ag daughter Martha, age 13
1920 - 1930		
	1925	Beverly Beach Resort is opened by Edgar Kalb, a successful Baltimore attorney
	January 24th, 1928	William A. Emmans marries Viola L. Carlisle at the age of 26
	1928	Reverand Emmans becomes the pastor of Maryland Avenue Baptist Church
	April 7th, 1930	Balitmore Census shows that Sylvan is 59 and Mamie is 52
1930 - 1940		
	1935	Sylvan Likes dies
	April 11th, 1936	Widow Mamie B. Likes sells 5.5 acres of land to St. Rose's Technical School of the Distric ot Columbia
	May 2nd, 1936:	Widow Mamie Likes Sells 4.7 acres of land to Madeline Tuck (probably the Miatticos home as Dr. Choate recalls)
	April 6th, 1940:	Widow Mamie B. Likes sells 12 acres of land to Sisters of Charity of St. Josephs
	1941	A property was purchased by Reverand Emmans and his wife Viola by selling their summer cottage at Shoreham B They purchased a summer camp property called "Callawasse" on the Rhode River, which contained 10 log cabins a
	October 15th, 1947	St. Rose's Technical School of the district of Columbia sells land to Sisters of Charity of St. Josephs
1940 - 1950		
	1944	Mamie B. Likes dies
1950 - 1960		
	May 9th, 1953	Sisters of Charity of St. Josephs sells land to Wabanna Bible Conference Association with a $10 down payment an cost of $135.000
	1956	The "Century Club" began, founded by Reverand Emmans. Members agreed to donate $100 to camp every year.
	50's	*These items were added: The new Snack Shop, the Rec Hall, Harmony Hall, and the stone Sea Wall*
1960 - 1970		
	1964	Maryland Avenue Baptist Church moved to a new location

1968	Richard Kalb closed down Beveryly Beach because the courts had ordered him to dessegregate
60's	*These items were added: The Key House, Miniature Golf, the Family Cottage, the Swimming Pool*

1970 - 1980

Sunday, August 12th, 1979	Sister Isabel Toohey dies; she is the signer of the sales transaction from the Catholic church to Reverand Emmans
70's	*These items were added: The brick cottage (house on main road)*

1980 - 1990

September, 1987	William A. Emmans dies
80's	*These items were added: The vinyl siding on the Lodge, the sewage line and county pier*

1990 - 2000

90's	The two Dorms, first named Dorm 1 and Dorm 3 were built
	HVAC was installed in the Lodge

2000 - 2010

May 6th, 2002	Robert C. "Bob" Emmans dies
2004	Mark Bates takes over as Executive Director
00's	*These items were added: The new sea wall, Geo-Thermal heating in the Lodge*

2010 - 2020

2014	Neal Luebbers takes over as Executive Director
2014	Owen Farmhouse is completed; opened and used for the first time that summer
March 25th, 2016	Yvonne Emmans dies
10's	*These items were added: The Pavilion, the new "Sport Court", Owen Farmhouse, additions to two townhouses*

THE POCKET TESTAMENT LEAGUE

Virtual Museum

On December 7, 1941 Japanese bombers dive onto Pearl Harbor, led by Captain Mitsuo Fuchida, who would later be led to Christ by League members. He is shown at right with Glenn Wagner. Click to read his story in his own words.

ABOUT THE AUTHOR

Mr. Frye has been involved with Camp Wabanna as a camper, counselor, dish washer, chapel speaker, and friend of the men and women who supported this ministry in the early years.

Sherry Tucker has always been a voracious reader and loves studying scripture. She and her husband have one son. He and his wife have given them three grandchildren that they regularly spoil. Sherry tries to balance cleaning up after their visits with reading and writing; she has not yet managed to succeed but will continue the fight. She was honored to help Mr. Frye in organizing this book and learned so much about Camp Wabanna in the process. Sherry Wynne Tucker is the co-author of "A Portrait of Obedience."

Printed in the United States
by Baker & Taylor Publisher Services